Questions and Answers: Countries

South Africa

A Question and Answer Book

by Kremena Spengler

Consultant:
Erla P. Heyns, Ph.D.
Director, Flower-Sprecher Veterinary Library
Cornell University

Capstone press®

Mankato, Minnesota

Fact Finders is published by Capstone Press
151 Good Counsel Drive, P.O. Box 669, Mankato, Minnesota 56002.
www.capstonepress.com

Library of Congress Cataloging-in-Publication Data
Spengler, Kremena.
    South Africa : a question and answer book / by Kremena Spengler.
    p. cm.—(Fact finders. Questions and answers. Countries)
    Summary: "Describes the geography, history, economy, and culture of South Africa in a
question-and-answer format"—Provided by publisher.
    Includes bibliographical references and index.
    ISBN–13: 978–0–7368–6411–4 (hardcover)
    ISBN–10: 0–7368–6411–3 (hardcover)
    1. South Africa—Juvenile literature. I. Title. II. Series.
DT1719.S7 2007
968—dc22   2006005057

Editorial Credits
Silver Editions, editorial, design, and production; Kia Adams, set designer; Ortelius Design,
    Inc., cartographer; Jo Miller, photo researcher; Scott Thoms, photo editor

Photo Credits
Afripics, cover (background), 7; Art Directors/Brian Seed, 25; Art Directors/Dave
Saunders, 11, 15; Art Directors/Martin Barlow, 12, 13; Bruce Coleman Inc./D. Robert
Franz, 1; Bruce Coleman Inc./Gary Schultz, 4; Corbis/Caroline Penn, cover (foreground);
Corbis/Charles O'Rear, 9; Corbis/Kim Ludbrook, 23; Cory Langley, 27; Getty Images
Inc./Touchline Photo, 19; One Mile Up, Inc., 29 (flag); Photo Courtesy of Paul Baker,
29 (coins); Peter Arnold/Roger De La Harpe, 20; Peter Arnold/Wolfgang Schmidt, 17;
Photodisc, 6; Root Resources/Byron Crader, 21; Photo Courtesy of Richard Sutherland,
29 (bill); Shutterstock/Marianne Venegoni, 18; Shutterstock/Richard Abram Sargeant, 16;
Shutterstock/Tihis, 24

1 2 3 4 5 6 11 10 09 08 07 06

Table of Contents

Features

Where is South Africa?

South Africa lies on the southern tip of the African continent. It is about twice as large as the U.S. state of Texas.

South Africa's land is varied. A wide, grassy **plateau** takes up most of the inland. Mountains rise along the plateau's edge on the west, south, and east. Narrow lowlands run along the coast.

Zebra and wildebeest roam the South African grasslands.

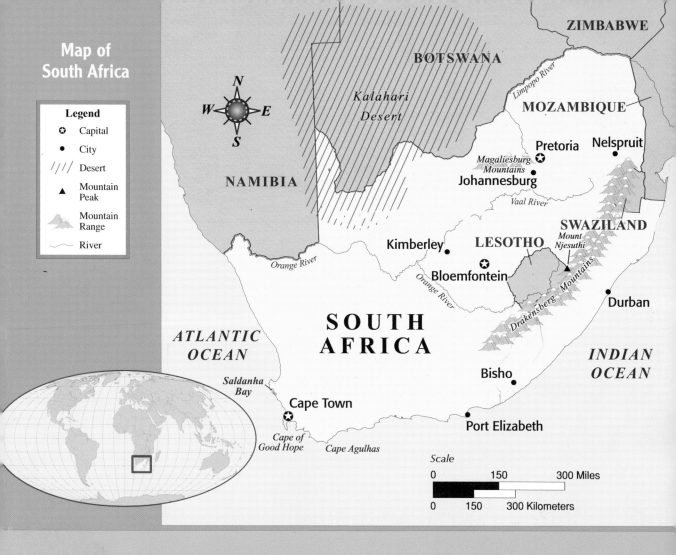

Map of South Africa

Legend
- ✪ Capital
- • City
- //// Desert
- ▲ Mountain Peak
- 🏔 Mountain Range
- 〰 River

Inland weather varies little from north to south. It is warm, sunny, and dry.

The east and west coasts have different weather. The warm Indian Ocean makes the east coast hot and wet. The cold Atlantic Ocean cools off the west coast.

When did South Africa become a country?

South Africa became a country on May 31, 1910. But its history goes back thousands of years. The Bantu people settled in the area 1,500 years ago.

In 1652, the Dutch settled the Cape of Good Hope. German and French settlers followed. These white settlers became known as **Afrikaners**. When the British arrived in 1795, they fought with the Afrikaners and the native Africans.

Fact!

Nelson Mandela was in prison for almost 30 years while leading the struggle against apartheid. He was finally released in 1990 and continued to work hard for equality. In 1994, South Africans elected Mandela as their first black president.

Nelson Mandela celebrates his victory during the 1994 election.

In 1910, the British formed the Union of South Africa. But conflicts continued. In 1948, Afrikaners took power and **apartheid** began. Blacks were forced into areas separate from whites. The African National Congress, with Nelson Mandela as its leader, led the struggle against apartheid. In the 1990s, apartheid came to an end.

What type of government does South Africa have?

South Africa is a **democratic** republic. All people ages 18 and over have the right to vote. South Africans vote for a party. The party that wins the most votes receives the most seats in **parliament**.

Parliament is made up of the National Assembly and the National Council of **Provinces**. The National Assembly makes laws. The National Council of Provinces makes decisions on laws that have to do with the provinces.

Fact!

Each branch of South Africa's government serves in a different city. The executive branch meets in Pretoria. The legislative center is Cape Town, and the judicial center is Bloemfontein. That's why South Africa has three capital cities.

South Africa's National Assembly has 400 members.

The National Assembly chooses a president who serves for five years. The president acts as commander-in-chief and signs bills into law. The president also names advisors, called the **cabinet**, to help him.

What kind of housing does South Africa have?

During apartheid, people of different races had to live in neighborhoods set aside for their race. Most of South Africa's wealthy citizens were white, which was reflected in their homes. Homes in former white areas still have beautiful gardens and swimming pools. People with less money live in simpler brick or cement houses, or in high-rise apartments.

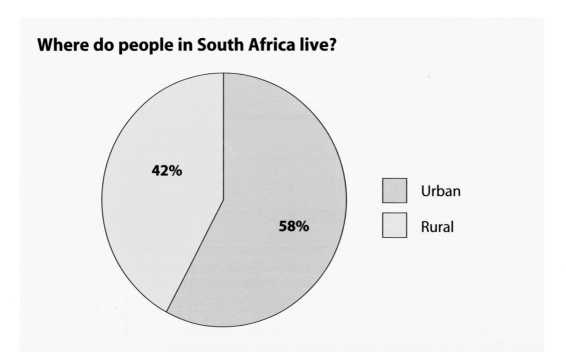

Where do people in South Africa live?

42%

58%

Urban

Rural

Although apartheid has ended, Mamelodi, a township outside of Pretoria, is still a mostly black and poor community.

The limited opportunities for blacks under apartheid was reflected in their homes. Today, many former black neighborhoods still have no electricity, water, or toilets. The poorest people live in tiny shacks. These shacks are made of cardboard, metal sheets, or even bottles and cans.

What are South Africa's forms of transportation?

South Africans built one of the longest road systems in Africa. Modern highways link cities throughout the country.

Many South Africans use public transportation to travel to work. Large buses and trains connect cities with the countryside.

Minibus tours are popular in Johannesburg.

Planes fly from Johannesburg International Airport to cities all over the world.

South Africa is a center for international transport. Most flights to southern African countries go through South Africa. The country also lies in the middle of ship routes and has some of the most modern ports on the continent.

What are South Africa's major industries?

For many years, gold mining was South Africa's most important industry. The country has half of the world's gold reserves.

South Africa is also a leading producer of platinum, diamonds, chromium, and uranium. Mines have provided materials to develop the steel and chemical industries. Mining and manufacturing wealth has led to the growth of finance and banking industries.

What does South Africa import and export?

Imports	Exports
machines and equipment	gold
chemicals	diamonds
oil products	platinum
scientific instruments	other metals and minerals
food	machines and equipment

Men drill in a gold mine in the North West Province of South Africa.

Farming is less important to South Africa's economy but is still productive. Farmers grow wheat and corn. They raise cattle and sheep. They also grow grapes and make world-famous wines.

What is school like in South Africa?

Children in South Africa must attend school until ninth grade. They study languages, math, and other subjects.

From ninth to twelfth grade, some students train for jobs. Others takes classes to prepare for college. To go to college, students must pass an exam at the end of high school.

Fact!

Students begin to learn a second language in third grade. In addition to their home language, they learn English and must also study one of the country's other 11 languages. Most South Africans speak several languages well.

Young girls attend a modern school in Johannesburg.

Schools vary widely. Some schools have modern buildings with computers, hockey fields, indoor gyms, and swimming pools. Others have no water, no toilets, and no telephones. A teacher in a poor school may teach up to 50 students in one classroom.

What are South Africa's sports and games?

Soccer is very popular in South Africa. Children play soccer in parks, streets, or any other open spaces. Both children and adults cheer for South Africa's national soccer team. South Africans lovingly call the team "Bafana, Bafana." It means "the boys, the boys" in isiZulu. In 1996, the team won the African Nations Cup. It also played for the World Cup in 1998 and 2002.

Fact!

Each year, some of the world's top golfers compete in the Sun City Million Dollar Golf Challenge in South Africa. The event has the largest prize in world golf.

South Africans, in white uniforms, play a team from the Democratic Republic of Congo in a soccer match.

South Africans also love rugby and cricket. Rugby is similar to American football. It is also played in Europe and Australia. The South African rugby team won the World Cup in 1995. Cricket is similar to baseball. It was invented in England over 700 years ago.

What are the traditional art forms in South Africa?

Music is an important art form in South Africa. In the 1930s, blacks in cities created *marabi* music. A voice would sing a tune as drums and pebble-filled cans measured the beat. *Marabi* was a way to protest against apartheid.

South African music combines the traditions of different groups. In the 1960s, "Cape jazz" mixed African, Asian, and other sounds.

Fact!

South Africa's first people, the San, left behind rock paintings of animals and people. It is the largest collection of Stone Age art in the world.

Traditional Zulu masks are hand-carved out of wood and painted in bright colors.

Local traditions are also seen in crafts. The **Zulu** weave colorful beads into bracelets, necklaces, and clothing. Different colors stand for "love," "being true," or other ideas. Other craftsmen make wooden masks, baskets, and clay pots.

What holidays do South Africans celebrate?

Many holidays in South Africa celebrate the struggle against apartheid. During these holidays, offices and schools close. Youth Day, June 16, celebrates students who fought against apartheid.

South Africa's national holiday is Freedom Day, April 27. April 27, 1994, was the first time South Africans of any color could vote.

What other holidays do people in South Africa celebrate?

New Year's Day
Human Rights Day
Good Friday
Workers Day
National Women's Day
Heritage Day
Christmas Day
Day of Good Will

Children release doves in a schoolyard during a Youth Day Celebration.

Some holidays mark other events. On Reconciliation Day, December 16, people remember wars between the Zulu and Afrikaners in the 1830s. It is a day of unity.

What are the traditional foods of South Africa?

South African dishes come from many traditions. In the 1600s, Indonesian slaves served as cooks in white homes. *Bobotie, sosaties,* and other Indonesian dishes became part of local cooking. *Bobotie* is a baked pot pie. *Sosaties* are mutton or pork skewers with small onions.

Indians who settled near Durban brought curries from India. These spicy casseroles are made of vegetables, rice, and meat.

Fact!

Local fruit are an important part of the South African diet. Grapes, apples, and pears grow in the Cape. Papayas, avocados, and mangos grow in the southeast.

Bobotie *is made with ground beef, eggs, onions, tomatoes, milk, lemon juice, and spices.*

The *braai*, or barbecue, is a special South African tradition started by Afrikaner farmers. People grill food in backyards and parks. A mutton and beef sausage called *boerewors* is usually part of the *braai*.

What is family life like in South Africa?

Wealthier families in South Africa live comfortably. In their spare time, families *braai* in the backyard, or go to the park, mall, or movies.

The life of poor families is hard. They cannot afford good housing. They have no water, sewer, and other services.

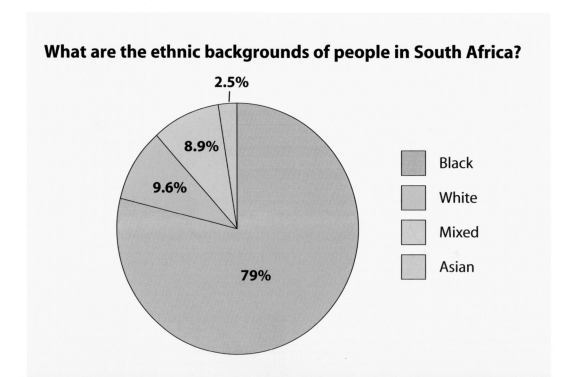

What are the ethnic backgrounds of people in South Africa?

2.5%
8.9%
9.6%
79%

Black
White
Mixed
Asian

In poorer areas, men have to take jobs in cities. Women are often responsible for raising children.

In many black farm areas, land is not suitable to grow crops. Men take jobs in cities or on mines. They may be away from their families for months. Women often raise children by themselves.

South Africa Fast Facts

Official name:

Republic of South Africa

Land area:

*471,008 square miles
(1,219,912 square
kilometers)*

**Average annual
precipitation (Pretoria):**

2.74 inches (69.5 millimeters)

**Average January
temperature (Pretoria):**

*84.2 degrees Fahrenheit
(29 degrees Celsius)*

**Average July
temperature (Pretoria):**

*68 degrees Fahrenheit
(20 degrees Celsius)*

Population:

44,344,136 people

Capital cities:

*Pretoria, Cape Town,
Bloemfontein*

Languages:

*11 official languages
including isiZulu, isiXhosa,
Afrikaans and English*

Natural resources:

*gold, platinum, diamonds,
chromium, manganese,
uranium, copper, silver, coal*

Religions:

Christian (Catholic and Protestant)	*79.7 %*
Islam	*1.5 %*
Other	*3.7 %*
None	*15.1 %*

Money and Flag

Money:

South Africa's money is the rand. One rand has 100 cents. In 2006, one U.S. dollar equaled 6.3 rands. One Canadian dollar equaled 5.4 rands.

Flag:

The South African flag has six colors: red, blue, green, black, yellow, and white. These colors have appeared on South African flags in the past. They mean different things to different people. The green begins as a "V" at the flag post, comes together at the center of the flag, and continues as a single band to the outer end. This shape stands for the unity of all South Africans. This flag became official on April 27, 1994.

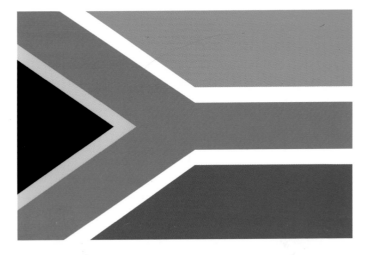

Learn to Speak isiZulu

Most people in South Africa speak English. The largest group, about a quarter of all South Africans, speaks isiZulu as its first language. Learn to speak some isiZulu words using the chart below.

English	IsiZulu	Pronunciation
hello	sawubona	sah-woo-BOH-nah
good bye	sala kahle	SAH-lah KAH-lee
yes	yebo	YAY-boh
no	cha	KAH
please	ake	AH-kay
thank you	ngiyabonga	ngee-yah-BOHNG-ah
boy	umfana	oom-FAH-nah
girl	intombazana	in-tohm-bah-ZAH-nah

Glossary

Afrikaners (Af-ruh-KAH-nurz)—relatives of the first white settlers of South Africa

apartheid (uh-PART-hate)—the practice of keeping people of different races apart

cabinet (KAB-ih-net)—a group of government ministers that help run a country

democratic (dem-uh-KRAT-ik)—belonging to a system in which people vote for their leaders

parliament (PAR-luh-muhnt)—the group of people who have been elected to make laws in some countries

plateau (pla-TOH)—an area of high, flat land

province (PROV-uhnss)—a district or a region of some countries

Zulu (ZOO-loo)—a member of the largest group of black South Africans

Internet Sites

FactHound offers a safe, fun way to find Internet sites related to this book. All of the sites on FactHound have been researched by our staff.

Here's how:
1. Visit *www.facthound.com*
2. Choose your grade level.
3. Type in this book ID **0736864113** for age-appropriate sites. You may also browse subjects by clicking on letters, or by clicking on pictures and words.
4. Click on the **Fetch It** button.

FactHound will fetch the best sites for you!

Read More

Blauer, Ettagale, and Jason Lauré. *South Africa.* Enchantment of the World. New York: Children's Press, 2006.

Britton, Tamara L. *South Africa.* Checkerboard Geography Library: The Countries. Edina, Minn.: Abdo, 2003.

Finlayson, Reggie. *Nelson Mandela.* Just the Facts Biographies. Minneapolis: Lerner, 2006.

Graham, Ian. *South Africa.* Country File. North Mankato, Minn.: Smart Apple Media, 2005.

Index